Medal group of Captain H. Trevor, 15th Sikhs: Egypt, undated, clasps 'Suakin 1885' and 'Tofrek'; India General Service Medal (IGS) 1854, clasp 'Burma 1887–89'; IGS 1895, clasps 'Punjab Frontier 1897–98' and 'Tirah 1897–98'; Khedive's Star dated 1884–6. At far right is the bronze Royal Humane Society Medal for gallantry in saving life.

BRITISH CAMPAIGN MEDALS 1815–1914

Peter Duckers

The Shire Book

Published in 2004 by Shire Publications Ltd,
Cromwell House, Church Street, Princes Risborough,
Buckinghamshire HP27 9AA, UK.
(Website: www.shirebooks.co.uk)

Copyright © 2000 by Peter Duckers.
First published 2000; reprinted 2004.
Shire Album 384. ISBN 0 7478 0465 6
Peter Duckers is hereby identified as the author of this
work in accordance with Section 77 of the Copyright,
Designs and Patents Act 1988.

British Library Cataloguing in Publication Data:
Duckers, Peter
British campaign medals 1815–1914.
– (The Shire book)
1. Great Britain. Army – Medals, badges,
decorations, etc.
2. Great Britain. Royal Navy – Medals, badges,
decorations, etc.
I. Title 355.1'342'0941
ISBN 0 7478 0465 6

Cover: *Medal group to a sailor: Baltic Medal (1854–5); Crimean War Medal with clasps
'Inkermann' and 'Sebastopol'; Naval Long Service and Good Conduct medal; Turkish Crimea Medal
(British reverse).*

ACKNOWLEDGEMENTS
The author would like to thank Mr Paul Davies, photographer to Shrewsbury Museums
Service, for taking many of the photographs.

Printed in Great Britain by CIT Printing Services Ltd,
Press Buildings, Merlins Bridge, Haverfordwest,
Pembrokeshire SA61 1XF.

Contents

Honourable East India Company medal for the capture of the island of Java, 1811.

Introduction

The idea of giving medals to soldiers for war service goes back to antiquity – certainly to Roman times. In Britain the first were awarded in very small numbers for the Armada campaign of 1588 and thereafter only sparingly during the Civil Wars (1642–51) and the Dutch Wars. However, these and others issued during the eighteenth century were not campaign medals in the modern sense: they were often awards for gallantry to individuals or limited to a few recipients.

The Honourable East India Company (HEIC) began the practice of issuing general campaign medals, as a form of reward to its native Indian troops. From the 1770s onwards these became increasingly common as the company's power was extended by conquest. Examples of early HEIC awards are those for the Deccan campaign of 1778–84, the Mysore campaign of 1790–2 and for Seringapatam, 1799.

At the same time, medals were being issued by private individuals or associations, a trend which is particularly noticeable during the French Wars of 1793–1815. The ironmaster Matthew Boulton, for example, distributed medals to some of the participants at the Battles of the Nile in 1798 and Trafalgar in 1805, as did Alexander Davison, a 'prize-agent' responsible for distributing money made from the sale of captured enemy ships. Although these HEIC and private medals predate those officially awarded by the British government, they do not conform to the modern idea of a campaign medal – something awarded to *every* soldier or sailor who served within a designated campaign area, regardless of rank or distinction.

*Below left:
Honourable East
India Company
medal for the
Mysore campaign,
1790–2.*

*Below right:
Honourable East
India Company
medal for the
capture of
Seringapatam in
1799. It is in gold,
as awarded to
senior officers.*

British army uniform, headgear and badges of the 1880s. (Shropshire Regimental Museum)

Collecting campaign medals

The hobby of collecting British campaign medals began in the late nineteenth century. As the British Empire expanded, more and more medals were awarded for military service around the globe and, as these came on the market, the hobby itself grew.

Perhaps the greatest stimulus to collecting these awards – apart from the fact that some are very attractive in design – is the fact that the majority of British awards were named to their recipients, either officially (at the Royal Mint or the Calcutta Mint) or unofficially. Typically, the medal will give the name, rank and regiment of the recipient, usually impressed or engraved around the rim or sometimes on the reverse. This enables the collector to research the man himself or his regiment and to follow his career throughout his service or in a particular campaign or battle. With the growing number of reference

Medal group of Sir A. J. F. Reid, Indian Army: 1903 Coronation (India); Second Afghan War Medal, 1878–80 (clasp 'Peiwar Kotal'); 1854 IGS (clasps 'Hazara 1888' and 'Samana 1891'); 1895 IGS (clasps 'Relief of Chitral 1895', 'Punjab Frontier 1897–98' and 'Malakand 1897') and medal for the Third China War, 1900.

As they were issued: medals with their original labelled card boxes, as awarded to Lieutenant J. E. Mein, 5th Punjab Infantry, Indian Army. Left: India General Service (1854–95), with three clasps. Right: Second Afghan War (1878–80) with clasp 'Kabul'.

books, campaign histories, memoirs and battle studies now in print and the availability of original service documents (for example, in the Public Record Office, Kew), the diligent or fortunate researcher can put together a detailed file of information on the recipient of a medal or on the campaign. The medal thus represents a tangible, personalised link between the past and the present.

Collectors naturally vary in their interests. Some collect to a particular regiment, campaign, battle or geographical area (such as India), whilst others prefer medals to officers, particular ranks or individual ships, or collect medal *groups* rather than single items. Some collectors take the genealogical aspect of medal collecting one stage further and collect only to their own family name(s). As with any other hobby, what matters is that collectors suit themselves and find interest and diversion in the hobby.

Basic terms

CAMPAIGN MEDALS

Campaign medals are medallic awards for service in a particular military campaign or battle. They were given for being present within a designated area, without regard to the recipient's rank or achievements, in contrast to gallantry awards or decorations. Medals and clasps (see below) were made at the Royal Mint or the Calcutta Mint and were usually awarded within a year or so of the event they commemorated, although this could be longer if, as with large campaigns, the Mint had to produce many more medals.

The medals were distributed at formal ceremonies to men still serving. These could be very grand affairs (such as the Crimean War presentation in Hyde Park in 1855, when Queen Victoria herself handed out thousands of medals), but ceremonies could also be much smaller, such as aboard a ship with the captain officiating. Men who had left the services received their medals through the post. Sometimes it was difficult to award medals to men who had, for example, changed ship between campaigns, and there are records of medals following men around the navy until they finally caught up with them.

The principal parts and features of a medal.

Medals are worn in chronological order of award from the centre of the wearer's left chest outwards. Gallantry awards are worn on the left (as viewed) and foreign awards to the viewer's right. In cases in which

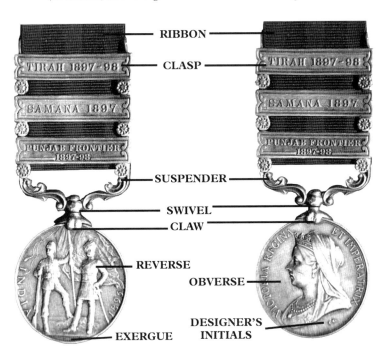

RIBBON

CLASP

SUSPENDER

SWIVEL

CLAW

REVERSE

OBVERSE

EXERGUE

DESIGNER'S INITIALS

Medal group of three featuring: 1854 IGS, for 'Jowaki 1877–8'; Afghan War Medal (1878–80), with three clasps; and East and West Africa Medal for 'M'wele 1895–6'. Three different effigies of Queen Victoria are shown.

dates of campaigns overlap, the date of the order authorising the award is taken as the date of precedence.

After Waterloo (1815) medals for soldiers or sailors who had died during a campaign, in action or from any other cause, were awarded to the next of kin. Sometimes the next of kin was not known and the medal was never awarded or a relative could learn many years later of a medal waiting to be claimed. One award for Azoff 1855 was not claimed until 1907 and another for Ashanti 1873 until 1937.

CLASPS

Clasps are commonly, though not strictly correctly, also referred to as 'bars'. They are single-faced metal bars carried on the ribbon attached to the medal, indicating service in a particular campaign (for example *Burma 1885–7*) or a battle (for example *Alma*). Most are plain and flat though some are distinctively shaped (such as those for the Indian Mutiny or the Crimean War). The clasps carry side flanges to enable them to be attached to the suspension (see page 10) and riveted to each other, so that new ones can be attached as earned. Sometimes the top flanges were clipped off. Usually the first-earned clasp is borne nearest to the medal, so that the latest earned should be at the top, but clasps are occasionally found in the 'wrong' order, perhaps because they were sent to the recipient individually at a later date and attached wrongly, often in a variety of 'unofficial' ways with wire and pins.

New collectors should try to be sure that the clasps on a medal are the ones given to the recipient and have not been added later, either by a soldier who wanted to claim more or for fraudulent purposes. On most awards to British troops the clasps are neatly riveted together along the sides. There was no limit to the number of clasps a man could wear on the appropriate ribbon – so long as he had earned them. It is said that the India General Service Medal (IGS) of 1854–95 was replaced by the 1895–1902 version because a General saw his soldiers with so many clasps but only one medal and thought this not a fair reflection of their years of active service.

MATERIALS

The majority of British medals and clasps are made of solid silver, though some were issued in bronze versions, mainly to Indian non-combatant 'followers' like grooms, servants and water-carriers. A few – usually Stars – were issued in other metals, such as bronze (Khedive's Stars) or gun-metal from captured enemy cannon (the Kabul to Kandahar Star). The majority of British campaign awards are circular, usually 36 mm in diameter.

RIBBONS

Medals are worn suspended from their own specific ribbons (or ribands). At first these were made of silk but cotton was increasingly used as the nineteenth century progressed. Their colours often have some heraldic or symbolic significance: the blue and white stripes of the 1882–8 Egypt medals, for example, are said to signify the Blue and White Niles, while the red and green ribbon of the Second Afghan War medal shows the heraldic colours of Great Britain and of Islam.

Ribbon widths can vary slightly but generally were set at 32 mm. Smaller ones include the Crimean War and Ashanti Star ribbons, wider ones the Ghuznee Medal and the Kabul to Kandahar Star. Later ribbons tend to show more standardisation. About 4 cm of ribbon was meant to show, but many with a large number of clasps would have been much longer and there never seems to have been a hard and fast rule about the length of ribbon.

Generally no two ribbons are the same but occasionally there are 'clashes' – the First Afghan War Medal (1841–2), the Scinde Medal and the bronze stars for the Gwalior campaign all had the same 'Sunrise in the East' ribbon, for example. At first the intention was that all medals for service in one area, for example India, should have the same ribbon, but this was later abandoned and the idea of an area medal, not ribbon, was introduced with General Service medals.

OBVERSE

This is the side of the medal bearing the reigning monarch's effigy and titles. These were usually designed by the Royal Mint's artists, prominent amongst whom were William Wyon (who also did the head on the 'Penny Black' stamp and on many coins) and his family.

REVERSE

This is the side of the medal bearing a decorative design. These designs often have a symbolic or allegorical meaning and often feature classical images ('Victory' on the Sutlej or Sudan medals, for example)

The 'young head' of Queen Victoria. Designed at the Royal Mint by William Wyon, it was used on many Victorian campaign medals.

or appropriate motifs, such as marching armies (the Second Afghan War Medal of 1878–80, the South Africa Medals of 1899–1902). Some early reverses simply bear the name of the campaign or battle and a date (Afghanistan, 1841–2, the Scinde Medal). Many of the designs were open to competition or tender and there were many different designers. The designer's initials or name are often found on the reverse.

SUSPENSION

This is the means of attaching the ribbon and clasps to the medal disc by a claw. Most British medals have swivelling suspensions allowing the medal to be turned around to show either side whilst still showing the correct side of the clasp. Medals were to be worn with the obverse facing the viewer (that is, with the monarch's head visible). The bar carrying the ribbon itself can be very plain (for example the Egypt medals; China, 1900; South Africa, 1899–1900), slightly shaped (as in the 'cusped' suspender of the Indian Mutiny Medal) or of the 'ornamented' type much used in the nineteenth century (for example on the India General Service medals or South Africa medals). Stars tended to have a simple ring suspension and were not designed to bear clasps.

EXERGUE

This is an area on the lower reverse of the medal, often bearing the designer's name or initials, or the dates of a campaign, or the name of a battle (for example the Sutlej Medal).

NAMING

Most British awards are found named to their recipient, which is what makes the hobby so interesting to collectors. The naming is generally found around the lower rim and was done by machine in impressed block capitals or hand-engraved in a wide variety of often very attractive scripts. On some early awards (for example the Ghuznee Medal, 1839) naming can be found on the reverse of the medal. Most medals were officially named at the Mint before issue and usually bear the recipient's rank and name, and regiment, ship or branch of service. Often the regimental number is given. Again, as the century wore on, standardisation of naming became more apparent.

When medals were issued unnamed (for example the Baltic Medal, 1854–5; the Ashanti Star, 1896) the recipients often had them engraved by a local jeweller, regimental smith or private engraver. There is thus a wide range of naming styles on some medals and the beginner needs to learn quickly which are appropriate to the medal and period, and which have been added to unnamed medals much later for fraudulent purposes.

The medals

THE WATERLOO MEDAL, 1815

After the decisive victory at Waterloo on 18th June 1815 the British government sanctioned what is generally regarded as the very first campaign medal. It was the first award to be given to every soldier, regardless of rank, present within a defined area; it was the first medal to be machine-named (around the rim) with the recipient's rank, name and regiment; and it was the first medal to be awarded to the next of kin of casualties during the campaign. Original issues had a clip-and-ring suspension for the ribbon, but many personalised variations are to be found.

The Waterloo Medal was granted to any soldier of the British army (including the King's German Legion) present in the campaign of June 1815 and who served in any of its actions: Ligny and Quatre Bras on 16th June, the retirement to Waterloo on the 17th and the great battle itself on the 18th. It was also given to soldiers of the Reserve Division at Hal and Tubize, who saw no action.

However, the grant of a medal for Waterloo is a reflection of the importance of the victory rather than any desire on the part of the authorities to establish the precedent of issuing medals. For many years after Waterloo it was the Honourable East India Company which took the lead in giving medals to soldiers simply 'for being there' on campaign service.

The Waterloo Medal (1815) is regarded as the first general campaign award. Note the original large clip-and-ring suspension. Far left: *The reverse design.* Left: *The obverse, showing the head of the Prince Regent (later George IV) ruling in his father's place since 1812.*

Contemporary print of the Battle of the Pyrenees, July 1813. In 1847 survivors could claim the Military General Service Medal and clasp 'Pyrenees' for this major action.

The Military General Service Medal for the French Wars (1793–1814). Awarded only to survivors, who had to make a personal claim, most of its clasps recall the battles of the Peninsular War (1808–14).

THE RETROSPECTIVE MEDALS OF 1847–51

The soldiers and sailors who had taken part in the wars between 1793 and 1815 received no official medals for their service. Not until the 1840s did public pressure for recognition of the survivors of 'the Great French War' lead to action.

In 1847 the **Military General Service Medal** (MGS) was inaugurated to commemorate active service with Britain's land forces between 1793 and 1814. It was awarded only to survivors, who had to claim the medal – and over 25,600 men did so. Twenty-nine clasps were authorised, with fifteen being the most awarded to one man. Medals with up to five clasps are the norm; more than ten would be rare.

Although intended to cover the campaigns of 1793–1814 (dated on the medal), the earliest clasp, *Egypt,* was actually for the campaign of 1801. *Martinique* and *Guadaloupe* commemorated fighting in the West Indies in 1808–9, *Java* in the East Indies, *Maida* in Italy in 1807 and three rare clasps – *Fort Detroit,*

The Naval General Service Medal (1847): the very attractive reverse of the medal, which commemorated some of Britain's greatest naval victories as well as campaigns around the globe.

Chateauguay and *Chrysler's Farm* – fighting against the USA in the war of 1812–14. The others relate to stages of the Peninsular War in Portugal, Spain and southern France between 1808 and 1814. Some clasps recall epic land battles – *Corunna, Talavera, Fuentes d'Onor, Barrosa, Albuhera, Salamanca, Vittoria*; others recall great sieges – *Badajoz, Ciudad Rodrigo, St Sebastian* – and some fairly minor clashes, like *Roleia, Sahagun* and *Benevente* (these last two also forming one clasp if the recipient had served in both actions). Other battles commemorated were *Vimiero, Busaco, Pyrenees, Nive, Nivelle, Orthes* and *Toulouse*.

At the same time (1847–8), naval veterans could claim the new **Naval General Service Medal** (NGS). Because of Britain's predominantly naval role in the French Wars, there were many more actions to record. No less than 231 clasps were sanctioned, with just under 21,000 medals claimed. As with the MGS, some famous battles were recorded: Nelson's great victories, the *Nile* (1798), *Copenhagen 1801* and, of course, *Trafalgar* (1805). Other fleet actions included *1st June 1794, Camperdown* and *St Vincent*. The medal reflects naval action around the world – Russia, the East and West Indies, the USA, the Mediterranean and elsewhere. Most of the clasps issued were for ship-to-ship engagements, small landing parties or cutting-out expeditions and some were awarded in tiny numbers to the few survivors by 1848.

Unlike its military counterpart, the NGS was extended to cover later actions – fighting against Mediterranean pirates in 1817 (*Algiers*), the War of Greek Independence of 1827 (*Navarino*), and finally operations off the Syrian coast in 1840–1 (*Syria*).

A final retrospective award, the **Army of India Medal**, was issued in 1851 to the survivors of the arduous campaigns fought in India between 1799 and 1826, although the earliest clasp, *Allighur*, was for an action in 1803. Such were the conditions of service in the East that there were far fewer survivors to claim this medal – only 4500, the majority with single-clasp awards. Its twenty-one clasps covered the Second Mahratta War of 1803–4, the war against the Gurkhas of Nepal, 1814–17, and the Third Mahratta War, 1817–18. The award was extended to cover the siege operations at *Bhurtpoor* (1826) and the campaign in lower Burma (*Ava*) of 1824–6. Some of the clasps to Europeans were awarded in tiny numbers to the few survivors by 1851. *Assye* (1803) commemorates what Wellington called his greatest victory;

The Army of India Medal: issued in 1851 to the few survivors of early campaigns in India, 1803–26.

The Maharajpoor Star for the Gwalior campaign (1843). Its 'sister' award, the Punniar Star, was identical, but with 'Punniar' in place of 'Maharajpoor'.

other notable actions were the siege of **Corygaum** (four clasps awarded), the **Defence of Delhi** (six clasps awarded), **Poona**, **Seetabuldee** and **Capture of Deig**.

CAMPAIGNS IN INDIA, 1840–50

During the early years of the nineteenth century the HEIC once again took the lead in issuing medals for its campaigns in India. The conquest of the state of Gwalior produced two bronze stars (made from captured guns) for two battles fought on the same day, 29th December 1843: the **Maharajpoor Star** and the **Punniar Star**. The conquest of the Scinde in 1843 led to the issuing of the **Scinde Medal** for the battles of **Meeanee** or **Hyderabad** (or **Meeanee-Hyderabad** for those present at both).

The two wars against the Sikh kingdom, the Khalsa, proved to be amongst the most difficult the British ever fought. The First Sikh War of 1845–6 led to the award of the **Sutlej Campaign Medal** for participants in any of its four main actions: **Aliwal, Sobraon, Moodkee, Ferozeshuhur**. The first action is named on the exergue of the medal itself and subsequent actions borne on clasps – the first time that this system of indicating battle service had been used, since the MGS and NGS medals had not yet appeared.

A renewal of hostilities in 1848 led to the Second Sikh War and the award of the **Punjab Medal**, with clasps **Mooltan** (for the siege and capture of the city), **Chilianwala** (for the bloody battle on 13th January 1849) and **Goojerat** (for the final defeat of the Sikhs in February 1849).

The finely detailed reverse of this medal shows Sir Walter Gilbert receiving the Sikh surrender. After the overthrow of their kingdom Sikhs went on to serve with distinction in the British-Indian Army.

Far left: *The Sutlej Campaign Medal (1845–6): awarded for the First Sikh War. The first action in which the recipient served is embossed on the reverse; others are borne on clasps.*

Left: *The Punjab Medal (1848–9) commemorated the final defeat of the Sikhs and the subjugation of their kingdom, the Khalsa. Sir Walter Gilbert is shown receiving the Sikh surrender.*

British officers in Rawalpindi on the North West Frontier in 1849.

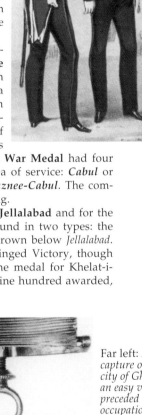

AFGHANISTAN, 1839–42

Because of its importance as a buffer state between the British-Indian and Russian empires, Afghanistan assumed a major strategic significance. The 'Great Game' was to prevent Russian control of India's frontiers and of Afghanistan and it drew Britain into two major wars in the nineteenth century.

The First Afghan War (1839–42) saw the capture of Ghuznee in 1839 (for which the **Ghuznee Medal** was awarded), followed by the British occupation of Kabul and Kandahar. However, a national uprising led to the notorious retreat from Kabul, in which a British-Indian army was destroyed with few survivors. A campaign of reconquest ensued in 1842 before British forces withdrew from the country. The **First Afghan War Medal** had four different reverses, reflecting the recipient's area of service: *Cabul* or *Candahar* or *Ghuznee-Cabul* or *Candahar-Ghuznee-Cabul*. The commonest is *Cabul*, but all reflect very hard fighting.

Medals were also issued for the **Defence of Jellalabad** and for the **Defence of Khelat-i-Ghilzie**. The former is found in two types: the first bore a simple reverse depicting a mural crown below *Jellalabad*. This was replaced by a version featuring a winged Victory, though many recipients retained the original issue. The medal for Khelat-i-Ghilzie is exceptionally rare, with only about nine hundred awarded, mostly to Indian soldiers.

Far left: *Medal for the capture of the fortress-city of Ghuznee (1839): an easy victory which preceded the British occupation of Afghanistan and the disastrous war of 1839–42.*

Left: *'Cabul' reverse of the medal for the First Afghan War (1839–42). This was actually awarded for the reconquest in 1841–2, which followed an Afghan uprising and the destruction of a British-Indian army.*

15

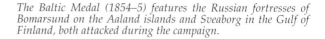

The Baltic Medal (1854–5) features the Russian fortresses of Bomarsund on the Aaland islands and Sveaborg in the Gulf of Finland, both attacked during the campaign.

THE RUSSIAN WAR, 1854–6

In 1854 Britain went to war against a major European power for the first time since Waterloo. The Russian War, commonly called the Crimean War because the main allied land campaign was fought on the Crimean peninsula, was actually waged around the world: in the Baltic and Gulf of Finland, in the Black Sea, in the White Sea to Russia's far north and even on Russia's Pacific coast.

The **Baltic Medal**, issued unnamed (apart from those to Sappers and Miners), was given to naval and Royal Marine forces engaged in blockade and landing-party operations in the Baltic and Gulf of Finland in 1854–5. The largest action was the capture of Bomarsund fortress on the Aaland islands (depicted on the reverse of the medal).

The **Crimean War Medal** commemorated some of the most famous – and infamous – military operations ever undertaken by the British army. The clasps *Alma* and *Inkermann* commemorate the defeat of Russian armies in pitched battle in the winter of 1854, while *Sebastopol* recalls the appalling suffering and the gallantry of British troops in the trenches before the Russian naval base, and their attacks on the Redan,

The Royal Navy in action: a gun-raft in the Sea of Azoff, Crimean War, 1855.

A contemporary print of the Highlanders attacking Russian positions during the Battle of the Alma, Crimean War, 20th September 1854.

the Quarries or the Malakoff. The most famous action, the Charge of the Light Brigade and the defence of Britain's naval base on 24th October 1854, is recalled by the clasp **Balaklava**. One clasp, **Azoff**, was awarded only to naval and Royal Marine personnel who served in the Sea of Azoff throughout 1855. The clasps took the novel form of oak leaves with acorns but this attractive design was not used again.

Allied forces also received the **Turkish Crimea Medal**. Those to British troops bear the reverse legend *Crimea* (British issue) or *La Crimea* (Sardinian issue); many British troops received the Sardinian version after the loss at sea of a consignment of the British type. There is also a French reverse, *La Crimée*.

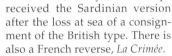

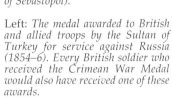

Far left: *The reverse of the Crimean War Medal (1854–6), showing the attractive oakleaf clasps (in this case for the battle of Inkermann and siege of Sebastopol).*

Left: *The medal awarded to British and allied troops by the Sultan of Turkey for service against Russia (1854–6). Every British soldier who received the Crimean War Medal would also have received one of these awards.*

17

British and French troops landing at Kertch in the Black Sea during the Crimean War.

An unnamed veteran wears his Crimean War Medal (with clasp 'Sebastopol'), the Turkish Crimea Medal and the Indian Mutiny Medal (with clasp 'Lucknow').

Medal for the Indian Mutiny (1857–9). Reverse, with clasps 'Relief of Lucknow' and 'Lucknow'. Shown with a typical (but unofficial) silver buckle to facilitate the wearing of the medal.

THE INDIAN MUTINY, 1857–9

The 'Great Rebellion' of 1857 began as a mutiny by Bengal regiments of the HEIC at Meerut in May of that year. British forces were initially taken by surprise by the spread and ferocity of the revolt: the garrison at Cawnpore was massacred, Lucknow, the capital of Oudh, was besieged and Delhi taken by the rebels. What followed was a bloody and difficult two-year campaign to reimpose British authority. The resulting **Indian Mutiny Medal** bore only five clasps – *Delhi* (for the siege and capture of the great city between May and September 1857), *Defence of Lucknow* (for the original defence force and the first relief force, which was itself trapped in the city), *Relief of Lucknow* (for the rescue and evacuation of the besieged garrison in November 1857), *Lucknow* (for the recapture of the city between November 1857 and March 1858) and *Central India* (for a series of arduous campaigns and battles under Sir Hugh Rose). Medals to the original Cawnpore garrison and to the naval brigades of HMS *Pearl* and *Shannon* are highly prized. Many medals were awarded without clasp but nevertheless may represent considerable action.

Indian veterans wearing a fine array of campaign medals, ranging from the Indian Mutiny (1857–9), through Abyssinia and Afghan War medals to the India General Service Medal of 1895.

MEDALS FOR SOUTH AFRICA, 1835–79

The growth of Britain's interest in the Cape route to the East and in the Cape hinterland led to clashes with South African tribes in the early nineteenth century. Several major frontier wars followed: in 1834–5, in 1846–7 and 1850–3. In 1853 the **South Africa Medal** was issued to those who had fought in one or more of these early campaigns. The date of institution, 1853, is borne on the reverse. No clasps were issued.

This medal was revived in 1877, with the date removed and a cowhide shield over crossed assegais (spears) in its place. The **South Africa Medal** (1877–9) bore a single dated clasp (*1877, 1877–78, 1878, 1878–79, 1877–79, 1877–8–9* or *1879*), awarded for service in a number of frontier wars, against the Galekas, Griquas, Basutos and Zulus. The most famous is that waged against the Zulus, January–July 1879. Medals to soldiers (mainly of the 24th Regiment) involved in the disastrous fighting at Isandhlwana on 22nd January and Rorke's Drift on the 22nd–23rd are particularly sought after and costly. The dated clasps were also awarded to sailors who served ashore in naval brigades; those who did not land received the medal without clasp, as did soldiers who did not cross the Zululand border in 1879.

Above: *The South Africa Medal (1853): obverse, with 'young head' of Queen Victoria. No clasps were issued, though the medal covered three separate campaigns.*

Right: *Medal for South Africa (1877–9), with clasp '1879' awarded for the Zulu and Basuto campaigns. Medals were issued with only one dated clasp, covering all the recipient's periods of service.*

THE MAORI WARS, 1845–7 AND 1860–6

The British settlement of New Zealand eventually resulted in clashes with the Maori inhabitants and two fierce campaigns were waged (1845–7 and 1860–6). The **New Zealand Medal**, issued in 1869 (over twenty years after the first campaign), had a dated reverse with six different versions for 1845–7 and twenty-two for 1864–6 and was only awarded to those who had seen action: naval forces, for example, did not receive the medal for offshore service (as they could with the South Africa Medal 1877–9). Dates covered the recipient's period of service in the various expeditions against the Maoris. Some dated reverses (*1847* or *1862–66* for example) were issued only in small numbers and are rare. Medals were also issued with no dates on the reverse.

THE CHINA WARS, 1840–1900

During the nineteenth century the British fought three wars against China, all aimed at securing treaty ports or defending trading concessions. The 'Opium War' of 1840–2 resulted in the issue of the **First China War Medal** with no clasps. It used a trophy-of-arms reverse, which was retained for all subsequent China War medals. Hong Kong was ceded to Britain as one result of this campaign. The **Second China War Medal** for 1856–8 (renewed 1858–60) saw a clasp for the naval action *Fatshan 1857*, whilst *Canton 1857* was issued for the occupation of the city. Attacks on the forts on the Peiho river resulted in the clasps *Taku Forts 1858* and *Taku Forts 1860*. The most significant action was the occupation of Peking and the destruction of the Summer Palace

Below left: *The New Zealand Medal for the Maori Wars. Undated reverse.*

Below right: *The trophy-of-arms reverse, used on all three medals for campaigns in China with date added for the 1900 campaign.*

with its irreplaceable works of art. **Pekin 1860** was issued to forces which took part in the capture and occupation. The **Third China War Medal** (1900) was awarded for the final Chinese campaign, caused by the 'Boxer Rebellion' – a nationalist uprising in 1900 which threatened foreign treaty ports and concessions. The rare clasp *Defence of Legations* was issued to the small embassy guard besieged at Peking for fifty-five days in 1900. Clasps *Taku Forts* and *Relief of Pekin* were also issued, the former to naval forces and the latter to British, Indian and naval units.

THE INDIAN EMPIRE, 1854–95

Inaugurated in 1854 for campaigns in India and on the fringes of the Indian Empire, the **India General Service Medal** (IGS) (1854–95) remained current for over forty years, with no less than twenty-four clasps being issued. It was in effect the first 'General Service' medal – one standardised area medal to which various clasps could be added as required or earned. One clasp, **North West Frontier,** was awarded for partici-

Below: *A Maxim machine-gun crew in India, c.1895.*

22

Above left: *The India General Service Medal (1854–95), reverse, showing Victory crowning an armed warrior. Clasps 'Hazara 1888' and 'Waziristan 1894–5' for campaigns on the North West Frontier.*

Above right: *Obverse of the India General Service Medal (1854–95); clasps 'Samana 1891' and 'Waziristan 1894–5' for campaigns on the North West Frontier.*

pation in any of seventeen frontier expeditions between 1849 and 1868, varying from severe campaigns (as in Waziristan in 1860) to relatively minor affairs (as on the Black Mountain in 1868). *Umbeyla* commemorates a particularly difficult campaign on the North West Frontier in 1863. Some very exotic expeditions are commemorated: *Pegu* (lower Burma, 1852–3), *Bhootan* (1864–6), *Naga 1879–80*. The clasps *Sikkim* (1888) and *Hunza 1891* were awarded for campaigns on 'the roof of the world' against possible Chinese or Russo-Chinese incursions. *Perak* (1875–6) was granted for operations in Malaya, and *Persia* for the full-scale war against Iran in 1857. A whole series of clasps rewarded those who had taken part in the conquest and occupation of upper Burma: *Burma 1885–7* for the initial conquest, *Burma 1887–89* and *Burma 1889–92* for anti-dacoit operations (against bandits) after the British invasion. Related clasps were *Lushai 1889–92*, *Chin-Lushai 1889–90*, *N.E. Frontier 1891*, *Kachin Hills 1892–93* and *Chin Hills 1892–93*, all for expeditions against tribes on the margins of Britain's new Burmese empire. Other clasps continued to record the difficult campaigns on the North West Frontier: *Jowaki 1877–8*, *Hazara 1888*, *Hazara 1891*, *Samana 1891* and *Waziristan 1894–5* (the last clasp issued to this medal). Many soldiers, especially in the Indian Army, received this medal with multiple clasps (seven being the largest number known to have been issued to one man) covering a wide range of campaign areas and dates.

ABYSSINIA, 1867–8

Perhaps the most unusual British campaign medal is the **Abyssinia Medal**, awarded for the campaign against King Theodore of Magdala in 1867–8. The expedition is regarded as a good example of careful planning and swift execution with minimal casualties to the forces under Lord Napier. The medal itself is very unusual, both in design and in naming. Each of the fourteen thousand recipients' details are embossed on the reverse – which meant that a different reverse plate had to be made for each soldier or sailor. This made it the most expensive British campaign medal ever produced, and the precedent was not followed!

CANADA, 1866–85

The **Canada General Service Medal** (1866–70) was awarded for service against American-based Irish-republican Fenian raiders along the Canadian frontier. *Fenian Raid 1866* was granted for operations against raiders who had captured Fort Erie and *Fenian Raid 1870* for later operations. The rare clasp *Red River 1870* was given to those who served under Colonel Garnet Wolseley in the river campaign against Louis Riel's rebellion. The medal was not authorised until 1899 and the majority of recipients were Canadian local forces, with only a few going to British soldiers or naval contingents on the Great Lakes. Some

The Abyssinia Medal (1868). Far left: *The obverse: perhaps the most unusual and distinctive design for a Victorian campaign medal.* Left: *The reverse, showing the recipient's details embossed. A separate reverse was needed for each of the fourteen thousand or so recipients!*

The Canada General Service Medal (1866–70), with clasp 'Fenian Raid 1866'. The medal was not issued until 1899.

16,100 medals were issued, most with one clasp. Medals with three clasps are very rare.

A new **North West Canada Medal** was issued in 1885 to Canadian forces who suppressed the second Louis Riel rebellion. One clasp, *Saskatchewan*, was given for those present in any of three main actions. Only 5600 medals were issued.

ASHANTI, 1874–1900

The process of imperial expansion in West Africa brought the British into conflict with the powerful Ashanti kingdom north of the Gold Coast (now Ghana). Three campaigns were fought.

In 1873–4 a British column drove Ashanti invaders from the coastal protectorate and crossed the Prah into Ashanti; after fierce fighting, the capital was occupied and burnt. The **Ashantee Medal** was issued for the campaign, with clasp *Coomassie* to those present in the final fighting and advance on the capital. The design of the reverse – a detailed jungle fighting scene – is regarded as one of the finest on a British campaign medal and was later adopted for other medals for East and West Africa and Central Africa.

In 1896, after a brief bloodless campaign, the Ashanti kingdom was brought under British control. The **Ashanti Star** was issued to the small force of about two thousand engaged. This unusual gun-metal star was issued unnamed, although awards to the 2nd West Yorkshire regiment were named at their Colonel's expense. The star was designed by Queen Victoria's daughter Princess Beatrice, whose husband, Prince Henry of Battenberg, died of disease during the campaign.

The final campaign against the Ashanti was a fierce affair, following an uprising in 1900. The British residency in Kumassi was besieged and a long and difficult campaign for its relief and the defeat of the uprising then followed. As Britain

The Ashantee Medal (1873–4), with clasp 'Coomassie'. The reverse is very finely detailed and was used for later East and West and Central Africa medals.

25

The Ashanti Star: for the brief campaign of 1895–6 against King Prempeh of Ashanti.

was already committed in China and South Africa, no British forces were available. The rare **Ashanti Medal** (1900) was granted for the campaign, with clasp *Kumassi* for those involved in the defence and relief operations.

AFGHANISTAN, 1878-80

A gun of G-3 Battery, Royal Artillery, on campaign in Afghanistan in 1879.

Britain became embroiled in Afghanistan again in 1878, with the Second Afghan War (see also page 15), which led to the issue of the **Second Afghan War Medal**. As before, the initial conquest went smoothly. Afghan defences at *Ali Musjid* and on the *Peiwar Kotal*

The reverse of the Second Afghan War Medal, showing a mixed column of British and Indian cavalry, infantry and artillery on the march.

were overwhelmed in November and December 1878 and British-Indian forces again occupied Kabul and Kandahar. A peace-treaty was agreed in 1879 but, as in 1840, the Afghans rose in revolt and the war was renewed. General Roberts's forces, fighting in the north, defeated the Afghans at *Charasia* (October 1879) but were besieged at Sherpur in December, earning the clasp *Kabul*. Sir Donald Stewart, fighting his way to Kabul from Kandahar, defeated the Afghans at *Ahmed Khel* in April 1880. Following a disaster to British arms at Maiwand on 28th August 1880, Kandahar was besieged and General Roberts led a column from Kabul to relieve the city. He defeated the Afghans at *Kandahar* on 1st September 1880 and the war effectively came to an end soon after. Those troops who had been on the march with General Roberts were given a special award, the **Kabul to Kandahar Star**, made of bronze from captured Afghan guns. The Second Afghan War Medal (1878–80) was also issued without clasp and in bronze, though the latter are rare.

Far left: *The Second Afghan War Medal (1878–80), clasps 'Ahmed Khel' and 'Kandahar'. Obverse, showing older effigy of Queen Victoria.*

Left: *The Kabul to Kandahar Star (1880). Awarded to troops who served with General Roberts on his epic march from Kabul to relieve Kandahar. Made from Afghan guns captured in the battle on 1st September.*

27

Above left: *The Egypt Medal, dated '1882', with three clasps: 'Alexandria 11th July' (for the naval bombardment), 'Tel-el-Kebir' and 'Suakin 1884'. An award to a sailor later serving ashore in the naval brigades.*

Above right: *A bandsman in Malta, c.1885, wearing the 1882 Egypt Medal and Khedive's Star.*

EGYPT AND THE SUDAN, 1882–91

In 1882 a British army under General Wolseley invaded Egypt, largely to protect British interests in the Suez Canal and its links with India and the East. The **Egypt Medal**, with reverse date *1882*, was issued to those who took part. Naval forces which served in the bombardment of Alexandria received the clasp *Alexandria 11th July* and land forces which served in the crushing defeat of the Egyptian army on 13th September received the clasp *Tel-el-Kebir*. Many medals were issued without clasp.

The **Egypt Medal** (with undated reverse) was revived in 1884 and 1885 for campaigns along the Nile and in the Eastern Sudan, around Suakin on the Red Sea. Since Britain assumed control of Egypt in 1882, it became embroiled in the problems of its protectorate, the Sudan, then in turmoil following the Islamic revolt by the Mahdi. A British force was sent to Suakin in 1884 and fought Mahdist tribes in a series of actions; clasps were issued to military and naval forces for *Suakin 1884* (for garrison duties around the port) and for the battles of *El Teb* and *Tamaai* (or *El Teb-Tamaai* for those present at both). The campaign

Relics of the Egypt and Sudan campaigns, 1882–5. (Shropshire Regimental Museum)

Right: *The undated Egypt Medal (1884–8), with clasp 'The Nile 1884–85' for the unsuccessful expedition to relieve General Gordon in Khartoum.*

around Suakin was renewed in 1885 and the clasp **Suakin 1885** was issued. **Tofrek** commemorated the largest action, fought on 22nd March 1885. A soldier or sailor who already had the Egypt Medal dated *1882* would simply receive the appropriate clasps if he served in a later campaign, not another medal.

In October 1884 a column had been sent along the Nile to relieve General Gordon, besieged in Khartoum. The column failed in its task, Gordon was killed and Khartoum fell to the Mahdi. Those present on the campaign received the undated medal with clasp **The Nile 1884–85**, whilst **Abu Klea** commemorated a particularly fierce action in the desert on 17th January 1885. **Kirbekan** was given for the battle of 10th February 1885, fought by the river column.

The undated medal without clasp was also given to naval personnel and to those engaged on the Egypt–

Receiving their medals: soldiers of the 1st Shropshire Light Infantry parade in Malta to receive the 1882 Khedive's Stars.

The Khedive's Star, awarded in bronze (with various dates) to British troops by the ruler of Egypt. Far left: The obverse. This one is for the campaigns of 1884–6. Left: The reverse, showing the Khedive's monogram. They are sometimes found named to their recipient on the reverse.

Sudan frontier. The last issues of the undated Egypt Medal were for two later actions near Suakin: the battles of *Gemaizah*, fought on 20th December 1888, and *Toski*, 3rd August 1891.

Soldiers who had earned the Egypt Medal of any kind also received a bronze star awarded by the ruler of Egypt in recognition of the part British troops played in putting down the revolt against Egyptian rule. The **Khedive's Star** was issued with date *1882* (for the initial Egypt campaign) or *1884* (for the Eastern Sudan) or *1884–6* (for the Nile and for the Eastern Sudan) or undated (for the 1888 or 1891 operations). Men received a single star for the first campaign in which they served. They did not get another for any subsequent campaign they took part in.

Above left: *The East and West Africa Medal, showing its 'veiled head' obverse. The reverse was the same as that for the Ashantee Medal of 1873–4. The clasp 'Witu 1890' was awarded for a campaign in East Africa.*

Above right: *The East and West Africa Medal with clasp 'Benin 1897', which was awarded to both military and naval personnel.*

MEDALS FOR EAST, WEST AND CENTRAL AFRICA, 1888–1900

The process of British expansion in tropical Africa after 1885 resulted in many small punitive expeditions or campaigns of conquest. In 1888 the **East and West Africa Medal** (EWA) was introduced, renewing the use of the 1873–4 Ashantee Medal reverse. Its twenty-one separate clasps commemorate a wide variety of actions. Some operations were large-scale affairs and involved British, Indian and local troops as well as naval forces. *Witu 1890*, *Witu Aug. 1893* and *M'wele* were granted for campaigns on the east coast of Africa; M'wele is unusual in that the campaign name is engraved on the rim of the medal, rather than borne on a clasp. *M'wele* (dated *1895* or *1895–6*) is the only occasion when the EWA is seen without a clasp. The largest operation was the campaign *Benin 1897* for the conquest of the kingdom of Benin. *Benin River 1894* and *Brass River 1895* recall earlier punitive expeditions on the West African coast. Rare clasps include *Dawkita* (awarded to only forty-one men for the defence of that village in March 1897), *Liwondi 1893* for an East African campaign and *Juba River 1893*. The most unusual campaign was that for *Lake Nyassa 1893*, where gunboats were brought in

31

Reverse of the East and Central Africa Medal for 1897–9, showing clasps 'Uganda 1897–98' and 'Lubwa's'.

sections from England, carried overland and then assembled on the shore of Lake Nyassa to carry troops on a punitive expedition. Many dated clasps (such as *1887–8*, *1892*, *1899*, *1900*) were awarded with this medal, often to very small columns of African troops for punitive expeditions in the hinterland of British territories; some of these are rare. *Sierra Leone 1898-99* was granted for service against a local rebellion, the Hut Tax War, and *Niger 1897* for a spectacularly successful series of operations along the Niger, in which small columns of African troops under British officers defeated large enemy forces.

The **Central Africa Medal** was awarded for a large number of small, but often fiercely contested, expeditions around the East African lakes; many recipients were Indian volunteers. The medal repeated the 1873–4 Ashantee Medal reverse. It was issued without clasp, with a swivelling ring suspension, for participation in one or more campaigns between 1891 and 1894. Those who served in one or more later campaigns received the clasp *Central Africa 1894–8*, which necessitated altering the suspension.

The **East and Central Africa Medal** (1897–9) was awarded mainly to Indian soldiers and African forces for campaigns in Uganda, largely against mutinous Sudanese troops. Clasps *Lubwa's*, *Uganda 1897–98*, *Uganda 1899* or simply dated *1898* were issued.

THE SUDAN, 1896–8

Having abandoned the Sudan to Mahdist forces in 1885, the British and their Egyptian allies began the reconquest in 1896. Several battles ensued, culminating (for British forces) with the defeat of the Khalifate armies by General Kitchener at the Battle of Omdurman in September

Far left: *The reverse of the Sudan Medal (1896–8): regarded by many as the finest design on a British campaign medal.*

Left: *The Khedive's Sudan Medal: as for earlier Egyptian and Sudanese campaigns, the ruler of Egypt awarded a separate medal for British and Egyptian troops engaged on the many expeditions into the Sudan between 1896 and 1899.*

The India General Service Medal (1895–1902), reverse, with clasps 'Punjab Frontier 1897–98' and 'Tirah 1897–98'. The clasp 'Tirah' is always seen in conjunction with 'Punjab Frontier', never singly.

1898. British soldiers received the **Sudan Medal** (1896–8), issued without clasps – another medal highly regarded for its artistic merits. Medals to the 21st Lancers for Omdurman are highly prized because of their famous charge, in which Winston Churchill took part, as are medals to the Royal Navy. Recipients were also awarded a medal by the Khedive of Egypt, which bore clasps reflecting battle service. British soldiers generally received clasps **Hafir** (19th to 26th September 1896), *The Atbara* (April 1898) and *Khartoum* (September 1898). Many other clasps were issued to the **Khedive's Sudan Medal** and to its successor of 1910, but these were mainly awarded to Egyptian and Sudanese troops under British officers for small punitive expeditions.

THE NORTH WEST FRONTIER OF INDIA, 1895–1902

In the late 1890s the North West Frontier of India erupted into revolt. In 1895 the small, remote garrison at Chitral was attacked and besieged. A new **India General Service Medal** (IGS) (1895–1902) was issued for this campaign, replacing the 1854 IGS. The rare clasp *Defence of Chitral* was issued to the small (mainly Kashmiri) garrison and its British officers; *Relief of Chitral* was awarded to the army which laboured through the Malakand and northern passes to relieve the fort. This clasp to the 32nd Sikhs is of interest, as they made a remarkable forced march from Gilgit in the east and relieved Chitral before the main column arrived. In 1897 the garrisons at Malakand and Chakdarra forts were attacked; the clasp *Malakand 1897* was awarded to the

Far left: *The 1895 IGS in bronze. Most medal awards for the Indian empire were also issued in bronze to non-combatant Indian 'followers' – cooks, servants, grooms and so on.*

Left: *The 1895 IGS with new obverse of Edward VII and clasp 'Waziristan 1901–2'. A new IGS bearing the head of Edward VII was instituted in 1908 (see page 37).*

defenders of either fort and the initial relief force. *Punjab Frontier 1897–98* rewarded service in any of a number of frontier areas under revolt, whilst *Samana 1897* was issued to those who had served in operations on the Samana Ridge. *Tirah 1897–98* was for the very hard frontier campaign of 1897–8. The last clasp to this medal, *Waziristan 1901–2*, was issued for a series of small punitive columns against the Mahsuds. The death of Queen Victoria at this time led to the redesigning of the obverse to this medal, to feature King Edward VII.

SOUTH AFRICA, 1890–1906

Cecil Rhodes's campaigns into the African kingdoms north of South Africa were rewarded with the **British South Africa Company's Medal**, which received official sanction. Few British soldiers took part in these campaigns, the majority going to local settler volunteer forces or the BSAC police. The striking reverse of the medal is the same in each case but bears the name of the campaign and date. Medals were awarded with reverse *Matabeleland 1893*, *Rhodesia 1896* and *Mashonaland 1897*. Men who served in more than one campaign received a clasp with the appropriate title and date. It was not until 1927 that a BSAC medal was issued, with plain reverse, bearing the clasp *Mashonaland 1890*; these are rare.

In 1899 Britain again went to war against the Boer republics of the Transvaal and Orange Free State. The British had been defeated in 1881 in the First Boer War but no medals were issued for this campaign. The war of 1899–1902 resulted in the award of two campaign medals. The **Queen's South Africa Medal** (QSA) eventually bore twenty-six clasps. Some covered areas of general service – *Cape Colony, Orange Free State* and *Transvaal* being the commonest, with *Rhodesia* and *Natal*

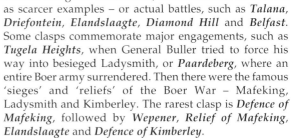

as scarcer examples – or actual battles, such as *Talana, Driefontein, Elandslaagte, Diamond Hill* and *Belfast*. Some clasps commemorate major engagements, such as *Tugela Heights*, when General Buller tried to force his way into besieged Ladysmith, or *Paardeberg*, where an entire Boer army surrendered. Then there were the famous 'sieges' and 'reliefs' of the Boer War – Mafeking, Ladysmith and Kimberley. The rarest clasp is *Defence of Mafeking*, followed by *Wepener, Relief of Mafeking, Elandslaagte* and *Defence of Kimberley*.

As Queen Victoria died in January 1901, before the war ended, a new medal was introduced bearing Edward VII's effigy on the obverse but with the same reverse. It was not possible to receive the **King's South Africa Medal** (KSA) without having already qualified for the Queen's, though it was possible to receive the QSA alone. The KSA was issued with only two clasps, *South Africa 1901* and *South Africa 1902*; a few men received the KSA with only

The British South Africa Company's Medal for campaigns of conquest in southern Africa. Although a 'Company' award, it received official sanction, though few British soldiers received this medal.

Officers and NCOs wearing a variety of medals including the 1854 India General Service Medal, the Second Afghan War Medal (1878–80), the Egypt Medal and the Khedive's Star.

one of the two, but these are rare. Nine clasps are the most to any one medal, with three, four or five being common. Unofficial awards were also issued for the siege of Kimberley (both a medal, now rare, and a silver star) and in bronze for the defence of O'Okiep.

A rare type of QSA has the reverse dates *1899–1900* in relief: since the war was expected to end with the fall of the Boer capitals in 1900, the medal was prepared for issue with those dates, but as the Boers continued a guerrilla war until 1902, the dates were erased. Only a few were issued with raised dates, largely to men of Lord Strathcona's Horse, a Canadian unit.

Another version of the QSA has *Mediterranean* in place of *South Africa* on the reverse and was awarded to militia forces called up for service in Britain's Mediterranean bases (such as Malta) to release regulars for the war in South Africa.

This medal makes a very interesting study, involving as it does British regiments (volunteers and yeomanry as well as regulars), naval contingents, local South African forces, and imperial contingents from, for example, Ceylon, Australia, New Zealand and Canada.

A medal was also issued for the Zulu rebellion of 1906 but the **Natal Medal** was issued only to local colonial forces.

THE AFRICA GENERAL SERVICE MEDAL, 1902

The **Africa General Service Medal** was instituted prior to the First World War but its use extended far beyond it – to 1956. Clasps awarded before 1914 were for small punitive expeditions or campaigns of conquest in East and West Africa. No fewer than thirty-four were granted for campaigns during Edward VII's reign alone. Three clasps commemorate service against 'the Mad Mullah' in Somaliland: the rare

The Queen's South Africa Medal. Far left: The reverse, showing its finely detailed design and with a selection of its twenty-six possible clasps. Nine clasps is the most found to one recipient, but these are very rare. Left: The obverse, showing the 'old head' of Queen Victoria, who died in January 1901, whilst the war was still in progress.

Below left: *The King's South Africa Medal, with its usual two clasps, and bearing the effigy and titles of King Edward VII, who succeeded on the death of Queen Victoria in 1901.*

Below centre and right: *The Africa General Service Medal (1902): clasps 'Somaliland 1902–04' and 'Jidballi'. The highly symbolic reverse design (centre) shows Britannia extending peace and law to Africa as a new dawn breaks. The obverse (right) shows the effigy and titles of King Edward VII.*

The medal for the Tibet expedition (1903–4). Reverse, show-ing the Potolai Lhasa temple-palace. This medal, also awarded in bronze, was given largely to Indian soldiers.

Somaliland 1901, then **Somaliland 1902–04** (with clasp **Jidballi** for the battle of 10th January 1904) and **Somaliland 1908–1910**. Many dated clasps were issued for the conquest of northern Nigeria (for example **N. Nigeria 1903**, **N. Nigeria 1904**) and punitive expeditions in southern Nigeria (for example **Aro 1901–1902**, and **S. Nigeria 1902–03**, **S. Nigeria 1905**); **Jubaland** was issued for the East African campaign of 1901 along the Juba river and **Nandi 1905–06** for operations against the Nandi tribe. Various dated clasps were issued for tribal operations in East Africa (such as **East Africa 1913**). The majority of the recipients (other than for the Somaliland clasps of 1902–10) were African or Indian soldiers.

TIBET, 1903–4

In 1903, in the last throes of the 'Great Game' (see page 15), a British force under Colonel Younghusband penetrated the largely 'unknown' mountain kingdom of Tibet from India and entered the capital, Lhasa, where treaty terms were agreed with the Dalai Lama. The **Tibet Medal**, with its delicate depiction of the great temple-palace, the Potolai Lhasa, was issued to British and Indian troops who were present. One clasp, **Gyantse**, was awarded to those who took part in the fighting around Gyantse fort in May–July 1904. The medal was issued in silver and bronze.

INDIA GENERAL SERVICE MEDAL, 1908

To replace the 1895 India General Service Medal, a new medal was inaugurated in 1908, bearing the head of King Edward VII – a change which should have been made for the IGS awarded in 1902 (see page 33). Before 1914 only two clasps had been sanctioned: **North West Frontier 1908** for either or both of the campaigns against the Zakkha Khel, in the Bazar Valley, or the Mohmands, north of Peshawar. The first was a swift

The India General Service Medal (1908). Reverse, depict-ing Jamrud fort in the mouth of the Khyber Pass.

37

Above left: *The obverse of the 1908 IGS showing King Edward VII in Field Marshal's uniform. Clasp 'North West Frontier 1908'.*

Above right: *The 1908 IGS, with obverse of King George V and clasp 'Abor 1911–12'. The medal (with new clasps as required) remained in use until 1935.*

and conclusive affair in Febuary and March 1908, whilst the latter saw more serious fighting. The second clasp, ***Abor 1911–12***, was granted for a difficult punitive expedition against the forest-dwelling Abors on the Burmese frontier. No British troops took part in this campaign. The medal with this clasp bore the head of King George V. The 1908 IGS remained current until 1935, further clasps being awarded as circumstances required.

Following up

Anyone who wishes to collect campaign medals should buy one or two basic reference books (apart from the regimental or campaign histories which may be required). *British Battles and Medals,* in its earlier editions by Major L. L. Gordon or in its 1988 version by Spinks, is an invaluable guide and essential reading. Alec Purves's *Collecting Decorations and Medals* (J. B. Hayward, 1983) is also useful. Militaria collectors' magazines and especially specific ones like *Medal News* (Token Publishing) or *The Armourer* (Beaumont Press) are useful sources of information and give details of dealers or fairs.

Information centres or libraries will give details of any local medal or militaria collectors' societies. National collectors' societies should also be considered: the *Orders and Medals Research Society* is the largest specially catering for medal collectors, but many others are relevant – the *Orders and Medals Society of America,* the *Military Historical Society* and the *Indian Military Historical Society* may all be of interest. Each of these produces a periodical *Journal,* which can be a valuable source of information and contacts.

Important medal collections are held by the National Army Museum (Royal Hospital Road, Chelsea, London SW3 4HT; telephone: 020 7730 0717; website: www.national-army-museum.ac.uk), the Imperial War Museum (Lambeth Road, London SE1 6HZ; telephone: 020 7416 5000; website: www.iwm.org.uk), and in many local and specifically military museums around the country. As there are about 150 regimental museums in the United Kingdom, most with fine collections of orders, decorations and medals, the reader is advised to consult *A Guide to Military Museums* by T. and S. Wise, which lists military museums, with visitors' details and contact numbers.

Although it is still occasionally possible to find campaign medals in local antique shops or markets, such finds are becoming rare. The serious collector will need to use specialist dealers' shops, dealers' postal lists or the major auction houses specialising in medals. Addresses and contacts are to be found in collectors' magazines and journals. Regular medal

A fine study of a sergeant wearing his Queen's South Africa, King's South Africa and Long Service medals, c.1905.

or militaria fairs are held most weekends all round Britain and are well worth attending.

USEFUL ADDRESSES
The Orders and Medals Research Society: Secretary, PO Box 248, Snettisham, King's Lynn, Norfolk PE31 7TA. Website: www.omrs.org.uk
The Military Historical Society: c/o The National Army Museum, Royal Hospital Road, London SW3 4HT. Telephone: 020 7730 0717.
The Indian Military Historical Society: Secretary, 33 High Street, Tilbrook, Huntingdon, Cambridgeshire PE18 0JP.
The Victorian Military Society: Membership Secretary, PO Box 58377, Newbury, Berkshire RG14 7FJ. Website: www.vms.org.uk

SOME LEADING DEALERS
(These issue regular sales lists to subscribers and attend weekend fairs.)
Andrew P. Bostock, Bostock Militaria, 15 Waller Close, Leek Wootton, near Warwick CV35 7QG. Telephone/fax: 01926 856381. Website: www.bostockmedals.co.uk
Philip Burman, The Cottage, Blackborough End, Middleton, King's Lynn, Norfolk PE32 1SE. Telephone: 01553 840350. Website: www.military-medals.co.uk
Peter R. Cotrel, 7 Stanton Road, Bournemouth, Dorset BH10 5DS. Telephone/fax: 01202 388367. Mobile: 07971 019155.
C. J. and A. J. Dixon Ltd, First Floor, 23 Prospect Street, Bridlington, East Yorkshire YO15 2AE. Telephone: 01262 603348 or 01262 676877. Website: www.dixonsmedals.co.uk
Spink & Son, 69 Southampton Row, London WC1B 4ET. Telephone: 020 7563 4000. Website: www.spink.com

AUCTION HOUSES
Dix, Noonan, Webb, 1 Old Bond Street, London W1S 4PB. Telephone: 020 7499 5022. Website: www.dnw.co.uk
Glendinings, 101 New Bond Street, London W1S 1SR. Telephone: 020 7393 3917. Website: www.bonhams.com
Spink & Son, 69 Southampton Row, London WC1B 4ET. Telephone: 020 7563 4000. Website: www.spink.com
Wallis & Wallis, West Street Auction Galleries, Lewes, East Sussex BN7 2NJ. Telephone: 01273 480208. Website: www.wallisandwallis.co.uk

Reverse of the India General Service Medal (1895–1902); clasp 'Punjab Frontier 1897–98'.